Leylah's Library: Channeled Writings of The Andromedan Council

Jameel Shaheed

This book is dedicated to the star child who knows no bounds, to the eclectic witch or wizard delving deep into the mysteries of magic, and to all who align with the star system Andromeda.

CONTENTS

Title Page
Dedication
The Experience of an Andromedan Starseed — 1
The Starseed is an Understated Miracle — 5
Are We More: Starseed Solitude — 7
Starseeds & Bloodline Trauma — 10
The Revolutionary & The Evolutionary — 13
The Realm of Peace (Home of Dragons) — 15
The Giants: Keepers of The Ancient and Bestowers of Faith (The Misconception & The Truth) — 18
Remaining Soft, Despite Hardship — 21
Jesus was from Sirius and Einstein was from Orion (Orion Starseed Transmission) — 23
Forgotten Realms of Consciousness (Intelligent Infinity Transmission) — 26
The Seer's Sanctuary — 29
Spirit World Residency (Merging With The Invisibly Infinite) — 32
Twin Flame Alchemy & The Path of Devotion — 36
The Book of Job & Self Love (Andromedan Starseed Transmission) — 39

The Night Light-Worker	42
Shhhh ,or Share (A Starseed's Need for Channeling)	45
The Path of Solace, & The Dark Arts Practitioner (Starseed Mission Transmission)	48
Enlightenment & The Journey Home	52
About The Author	57
Books By This Author	59

THE EXPERIENCE OF AN ANDROMEDAN STARSEED

"Your weirdness is your brilliance" - Steve Ahnael Nobel

Discovering one's celestial origins is a daunting task to say the leas.It is riddled with questioning, uncertainty, and confusion. Questions regarding the reality of the said experiences, uncertainty regarding our overall galactic placement, confusion as a sum of the initial questions and uncertainty. Yet I'm here to inform the other like-minded souls, that these experiences are very real, and embracing such is our saving grace.

I was brought onto my Galactic Family's Starship at the tail end of 2012. This experience has heightened my psychic senses, elevated my vibration, and affirmed my soul mission. Yet even with these profound gifts, it has been the hardest aspect of my journey to accept. In truth, to accept such is to accept just how "different" we are. To understand that despite appearances, our experience is very much outside the mainstream consciousness, as well as traditional spirituality. Yet it is in this understanding we find peace, as well as the answers necessary to persist in our soul missions. The most pertinent answer being, our Galactic Family.

This question has been at the forefront of my brain since writing my book "Tears Of The Dragon". I have written texts similar to this one many times, feeling connected to many star systems, primarily Lyra, Orion, Sirius, and Andromeda. In truth, this feeling of connection with multiple star systems highlights the work we do with various star races as a means to elevate the collective consciousness as a whole. Where our primary galactic families highlight our innate gifts, talents, and soul missions, our connections to other star races highlight our lessons being learned, as well as our overall synthesis with various forms of consciousness. It wasn't until 2020 that I came to know my Star Family, which is indeed, Andromeda.

It was in listening to a Collective Andromeda Starseed Reading by Tanya Master on YouTube that I understood that every one of my internal changes were connected to a collective of like-minded cosmic beings. That I was NOT alone in my personal expansion, and the best way to acclimate to my growth, is to lean into my peculiarities. To see ourselves as different is one thing, to see ourselves as unified in our uniqueness is solace.

Every Starseed can connect to multiple star systems, yet there is one that FEELS like home. Orion, Lyra, & Sirius we're all gateways to my home of Andromeda, a long journey to accept my celestial origins. This journey was particularly difficult due to the nature of The Andromedan Starseed. We are shape shifters, chameleons to whatever environment we are in, and though this ability is a gift, it can also become a coping mechanism and/or crutch, where we forget who we truly are. We can become people pleasers as a means to not "rock the boat", and though it is noble to seek amicable interactions, we cannot forget who & what we truly are in the process. We are Gatekeepers, Transformers, Keepers Of Time, Pathfinders, & Wayshowers for the Golden Age. It is our nature to learn all there is about others, including other star systems, by becoming one with their experience. We learn through them, yet find our way home to the frequency that resonates with our souls, Andromeda.

It is in understanding our nature, & our ability to BECOME whatever we are exposed to, that we learn the necessity to unplug from the collective as a whole. With time, we learn exactly HOW to engage the general public, as well as how frequently to do so, yet always finding time to retreat into our inner sanctum of cosmic consciousness.

As Andromedan Starseeds our NEED for solitude is a byproduct of our heightened sensitivity. This sensitivity not only warrants solitude, but HOW we spend our time alone. In truth, we are one of the more alien of the star races. I say that with love, yet it holds a seriousness despite jest. We are VERY SENSITIVE. We are unable to watch TV for extended periods of time, nor are we able to listen to solely lyric driven music. We must maintain a happy balance between television and meditation, between lyrical music, music based in instrumentation, and silence. So much love and our overall essence rests within quietude. We are also unable to engage in passion driven debates, and we are unable to work heavily time demanding jobs. Maintaining an objective scope when such debates arise, and knowing when to provide our perspective is essential. Our jobs should have a flexible format, where we can align our natural sensitivity to the rhythms of the planet, with a work schedule that flows with these invisible currents. In a sense, we MUST EMBRACE, the alien aspects of our experience to find solace in a busy, noisey, & dense world.

Most of my days are spent listening to high vibrational frequencies (this can include lyric driven music), communing with nature, trance meditations, and writings such as this one. Like I said, we are one of the more alien types of Starseeds. Yet I have come to understand that this is the only way to make sense of this world as a whole, and I know by doing so things become clearer for all who walk the planet. This experience is sacred, as well as personal, yet there is a unifying aspect within every change we endure. So in conclusion, I wish all who read this many blessings, as well as the courage to embrace the guidance of their star families. It isn't necessarily easy, yet it is necessary, and extremely rewarding. Signing Out, Your Andromedan Friend, Jameel.

JAMEEL SHAHEED

△△△

THE STARSEED IS AN UNDERSTATED MIRACLE

"True miracles aren't grandiose displays of power, rather a secret shared between friends"

Only Starseeds are fascinated with Starseed traits and transmissions. Own your uniqueness, reclaim your innocence, and explore the wonder within. People online don't seem to resonate regularly with your transmissions, this is fine. Perhaps your natural experience is within the higher realms, and your role as an anchor is designed to be invisible.

People will always be naturally drawn to your celestial wisdom within your living reality. The internet has the tendency to be a faulty medium for high vibrational frequencies. Do the things that make you smile, and provide comfort. How it feels will always supersede how it looks. Some souls are meant to be heard, others are meant to be felt. The latter are experiencing the 5D earth in real time, therefore nothing we do is less than miraculous.

Every interaction, every person we encounter, is playing an intricate role of the multiversal shift taking place. Anything we do is monumental, even if we are unable to see. The trick is to KNOW this as a certainty, and to model our 3D life around such a profound gift. Do what feels fulfilling, and freeing, for how it appears

JAMEEL SHAHEED

will never overrule the true magic that is taking place. Have Faith & Have FUN.

△△△

ARE WE MORE: STARSEED SOLITUDE

"The more powerful and original a mind, the more it will incline towards the religion of solitude." - Aldous Huxley

There's a certain level of solitude with any level of success. Whether this success be monetary, or perspective wise. In regards to monetary there becomes an apparent gap between one's achievements, and those seeking the same. In regards to perspective there becomes a large gap between one's level of consciousness, and that of his/her peers. Despite such, we begin to understand the necessity of the said solitude, as means to ground an experience most search for, or are unaware of.

It is in these private moments of solitude we cultivate our space, our ideals, our intellect, and our decisions. For in these moments of private contemplation, we learn HOW to conduct ourselves in the presence of those less fortunate. It is also in these moments we begin to discern the stark difference between ourselves, and our peers. We begin to see how the way our mind operates is completely unique to our disposition, yet is not separate to the overarching collective.

In fact, it is in these moments where we learn our role within The Divine Cosmic Play, and our impact on all within it's script. We begin to see the immeasurable ways others impact our decision making and character, as well as the countless ways the bridge between us creates the necessary link between what matters most. We begin to learn how to decide on what is most important. Not just for ourselves, but for the collective as a whole. We begin to learn the problems present in the lives of many, and find unique ways to provide guidance in such endeavors. We see how we are not solely independent parties acting on the behalf of instinct, yet are driven by higher thoughts, loftier ideals, and a purpose beyond the mainstream consciousness.

It is in these moments of embracing our aloneness, that we recognize our Divine Sovereign, and understand our importance on a cellular & cosmic level. It is in our solitude where we discover our driving force to persist. It is where we ask ourselves critical questions that only faith can answer. It is a driving force that stimulates the sleep AND the awakened, yet the methods in which we reach this conclusion differ in regards to our dispositions.

The primary question becomes, "Are We More?" We find answers to this question via our unique experiences, and understand the desire to ask such a question is what marks the stark difference between us and others. The answer is just as complicated as the question. The answer is rooted in knowing, as well as doubt. Yet the doubt is what sculpts our conduct, and allows us to understand who we truly are destined to be.

Modest Doubt is the beacon of the wise, yet when we receive even a glimmer of an answer, we must allow such to determine our behavior going forward. It is in solitude we ask ourselves the heavier questions, and also embrace the whole of our truth. Yet there is comfort in doing so, for we understand that there are many who share the same sentiment, and continually acclimate their behavior to uphold such a responsibility. It is in solitude that we recognize, hone, and enjoy our gifts granted by our unique place in the world. It is only in solitude that we can become all that we are, and answer the question, "Are We More?"

Given the fact that no human being while walking the Earth will ever know everything there is, whether this be sheer secular knowledge, or consciousness itself, there must be a force or "God" that operates within this said uncertainty. That in the space of incalculable probability resides SOMETHING that supersedes our level of awareness. In truth, we are speaking of God in a relationship to knowledge, yet there's still the question, does this source operate in a way that supersedes knowledge, and our level of awareness all together? I feel what most humans in general relate to as God, is honestly a level of awareness that some individuals currently operate from. With this being said, the individuals who recognize such have to model their behavior with this in mind. Yet for the individuals who ask these questions, it is understood that there is always something more.

STARSEEDS & BLOODLINE TRAUMA

"God wants you to be delivered from what you have done and from what has been done to you - Both are equally important to Him."- Joyce Meyer

Most Starseeds incarnate into darker bloodlines as a means to transmute generational trauma, and liberate the bloodline for future Starseeds. Even if this isn't experienced via their immediate family, somewhere within the bloodline darker activities were commonplace. The Starseed being as sensitive as they are sense this discrepancy, and oftentimes feel this energy within their experience whether it is being displayed by those they love, or not.

When it is present in the immediate family, Starseeds tend to stray from the company of their incarnated family, and seek their soul families to ground their experience. When it isn't present in the ones they love, this energy presents itself as an invisible sensation that oftentimes feels overwhelming, and confusing. The latter is more difficult to discern for the Starseed is unsure of why certain aspects of the psyche are being highlighted in their experience. They can feel at times haunted by something they feel they had no part in manifesting in their reality, and ask the question; "Why is my life so hard, what did i do to deserve this?"

Yet what the Starseed oftentimes forgets is that we are here in this incarnation for the exact reason we are feeling "overwhelmed". We are here to transmute the generational trauma of the said bloodline, whether the ones we are born to exhibit this behavior, or not. Our sheer acknowledgement of the trauma, and knowing that this trauma is not us, yet is here to be transmuted is a missing link in our Soul Missions. Starseeds re synonymous to invisible superheroes, where everytime we respond to non-love with love, a ripple effect is sent through the timeline, unlocking incalculable rewards for the bloodline itself. Yet, this isn't to say that this transmutation isn't met with resistance.

Oftentimes the ones who seeded the said darkness in the bloodline will resist the said transmutation in the form of Ego Attacks, and events designed to have the Starseed feel victimized and abandon their soul mission. Yet as I have, and continue to learn, if we simply understand that great transformations are coupled with discomfort and confusion, we learn unique ways to embrace the said trauma, and operate solely from our Higher Selves. With time we gain the ability to transcend perceived strife, and dance at heights the bloodline never thought imaginable. The key to this is to keep a still and empty mind. To know that when the mind is still it can be filled with anything, and when we respond with love and softness diligently, we are able to hear our Hearts, & Higher Selves communicate clearly, leading to more conscious and intuitive choices in our Earth Walks.

WE, are The Creators of our Realities. WE, are The Anchors of Unconditional Love, & Cosmic Consciousness. WE are The Unity, & Miracles Mother Gaia has called to service. WE, are The Silent Wish our ancestors asked for when things were the coldest. Practice faith diligently, love unconditionally, and know your weirdness is your brilliance and saving grace. Oftentimes, it takes the weirdest perspectives to transcend the darkest recesses of collective trauma.

JAMEEL SHAHEED

△△△

THE REVOLUTIONARY & THE EVOLUTIONARY

"The cosmos is within us. We are made of star-stuff. We are a way for the universe to know itself."- Carl Sagan

The Evolutionary Space supersedes The Revolutionary Space, yet each support the other in unique ways. The Revolutionary says "this is messed up, how can I change/fix this". The Evolutionary also acknowledges how distorted the situation is and says, "How can I make this work for me, and assist others in doing the same." Despite the perceived difference in approaches, both parties are working in tandem to liberate the human spirit. One just feels there is a more holistic, and self-preserving method to accomplish the said goal.

The Wise Revolutionary plays the "long game", The Wise Evolutionary plays the "deep game", understanding longevity is the only method change can occur. Much like nature The Evolutionary understands things happen slow or not at all, and is willing to take their time and live without certain "comforts" to achieve their end goal of liberation, and freedom. Where The Revolutionary may take chances at muddying the waters where morals are concerned to accomplish their objective, The Evolutionary knows their morals are how they add value, and will not compromise such in an effort to be "heard" or "remembered". They innately respond to their struggles with the value system they have cultivated over the years, and understand that the only way change can occur is to stand firm on these beliefs despite the challenges "the matrix" presents.

For the only way others can believe liberation is possible, is to see an individual constantly being who they are designed to be on a regular basis. The Evolutionary understands the only changes worth noting are the ones on the inside, for as they grow and EVOLVE, the collective does as well, even if these shifts are minor. The more willing The Evolutionary is to accept changes, trust their guidance, & persist in their journey, the easier it becomes for the next.

It is in catalyzing a collective effort that The Evolutionary finds solace in his work, and in turn, finds a peace that most yearn for. With all this being said, The Evolutionary and The Revolutionary support one another, yet their methods differ. It is essential these two parties bounce ideas off the other, and allow their value systems determine what is applicable to what must be done going forward. Allow all information to stimulate the experience within, yet don't diminish what has taken years to develop from an insight that may not be completely aligned with your overarching truth.

THE REALM OF PEACE (HOME OF DRAGONS)

"I do not want the peace which passeth understanding, I want the understanding which bringeth peace" - Hellen Keller

P eace as mankind has grown to know has always been a byproduct of war, or military exploits. It has been seen as an unattainable ideal that oftentimes fuels much destruction, or a monument on which foolhardy leaders seek their veneration. As a concept it has eluded even the greatest minds mankind has produced, yet it is in seeing it as a concept that has made it so elusive. Peace is not a concept, it is an energy, a frequency, and a 10th Dimension Emanation. It is a current that underlies the magical rifts throughout the multiverse, and it is a realm where the noblest of creatures call home; Dragons.

With this understanding, the image of the fire breathing, treasure hoarding monster dissipates from the psyche, and we begin to take a closer look at what Dragons represent. Dragons are understood as guardians, magicians, keepers of the ancient, and the wisest of council. Yet these elements of their nature are a byproduct of the space in which they operate. It is in being attuned to The Realm of Peace that these magnificent beings garner their allure, and timeless brilliance.

When we understand that peace is a vibration that echoes throughout time and space, we then understand just exactly what Dragons emit. There are many who recognize Dragons for their "power", yet a soul kindred to Dragonkind sees the dragon for its immense levels of love and compassion. A love so pure, and sacred, that what is perceived as "power", is honestly just a miscalculation of immeasurable compassion. This compassion has been cultivated over the aeons via The Realm of Peace. It is in this realm of the 10th Density, that Dragons represent the emanation that has been slipping through mankind's fingertips for ages. Peace is not a concept to imagine, rather a vibration to be felt.

Peace is centered within the heart of hearts, and blossoms from one's Solar Plexus Chakra. Like a bird fluttering, it is nestled within this area of the body, and as we sink into the solace of peace it constantly renews and refines our essence. It is an energy that can be tapped into at a moment's notice. It does not need to be chased, nor does it need to be suppressed in fear. It simply needs our nurturing, and belief. Belief that the vibration coined as "Peace" has no need for war. That as a realm of existence, it needs nothing more than our tender love and care. It is said that the path to peace is arduous, yet I disagree. It is in not seeing how bountiful peace already is that we make our journeys fraught with strife. If mankind only REMEMBERED that peace, much like magic is abundant within the landscape, we would understand how delicately sovereign a Earth Walk can be.

Yet given the current density of planet earth as a whole, we must take simple measures to access this realm of Cosmic Divinity. Everything to how we spend our time, how we engage others, and how we view ourselves, are dependent on our access to such a sacred element of being. To commune with Dragons and enter The Realm of Peace, man must first understand, peace is no concept, it is a vibration, and way of being. May blessings shower us all as we make our way home, and allow our understanding of peace govern the affairs we have moving forward.

THE GIANTS: KEEPERS OF THE ANCIENT AND BESTOWERS OF FAITH (THE MISCONCEPTION & THE TRUTH)

"Wisdom begins in wonder" -Socrates

If we were to cite the bible on the history and representation of those coined as "The Giants", we would get depictions of tyrannical monsters who brought mischief and ruin to all they encountered. They are depicted as a troublesome bunch who terrorized their fellow men, a group to be avoided, and ostracized. Yet as many of us have grown to learn, the spiritual history of mankind as we know it is very foggy. There is much to learn in regards to the true spiritual history of our experience, as well as much to uncover regarding the encompassing sanctity of our presence. Despite the overarching good religion has brought to the world, and to those who seek it's relief, the representation of what it encompasses has been distorted. For where many seek safe haven & solace within its truth, others have used it to fuel political and military campaigns throughout the ages...

The depiction of The Giants is much similar to that of the Dragons in biblical contexts, for where as monsters to avoid are painted, in actuality resides a fear of people gaining the knowledge to actualize their spiritual realization and identities. What these Cosmic Beings truly represented were the Keepers of Wisdom, and Guardians of the ancient ways of Lemuria & Atlantis. These beings in truth were equivalent to Librarians of The Sacred, as well as fierce protectors of The Ascended. Much how the depiction of St. George slaying the Dragon, is representative of the elimination of the ancient ways of Dragon Magick, the blasphemous depiction of The Watchers/Giants was an attempt to taint and monopolize the avenues in which humanity would seek spiritual fulfillment.

Despite this disheartening truth, as we enter this Golden Age, many souls are discovering their Cosmic Identities, Celestial Origins, and Soul Missions while walking Planet Earth. The truth is, THERE IS NO LIMIT in what we are capable of achieving, as well as the soul missions we are on this planet to fulfill. The individuals that align themselves with The Giants have immense levels of wisdom simply waiting to be tapped, as well as implemented. There is an innate desire to preserve the ancient, implement the ways of old, create storehouses of ancient wisdom, as well as guard and protect the sacred children and their Mother Gaia.

It is in recognizing the fallacies of history, as well as what is perceived as "ancient", that we unlock our Cosmic Divinity, and Soul Missions on this Earth Walk. Civilized history is dated around 4700 years old, and Giants are far older than that. Having a direct link to a Cosmic rhythm, that is far older than the rhythms of Gaia herself, and it is in this Cosmic link that Giants protect her, her children, and all the wisdom she holds. As Cosmic Beings, The Giants, are the keepers of the keys to The Akashic as well as the Primordial Magic of the landscape itself. It is in this responsibility that the misconception has arisen, for it is in the role as "Guardian" that many fear the wisdom within. Yet it is the role of Guardian that encompasses the energy of "The Giants".

Yet it is in this guardianship that we understand the necessities of gentleness and softness of being. The Gentle Giant supersedes the vain and ruthless rulers of this common era. It is in the docility of the Doe, the tenderness of the children, and simplicity of the elder we find our greatest strength. It is in these subtle moments of communing with the softness of spirit we come to love & appreciate the divinity of the human experience. As we grow in our understanding of the world as a whole, the many plights we face, and the preciousness of simply attuning to the frequencies of love and compassion, we become Bestowers of Faith for all we encounter. For it is in our faith in the immeasurable, our faith in the unnamable, and our faith in the heart of hearts, that we come to understand & appreciate our divine essence. It is no small feat to be a representation of all that is good in the universe. It isn't the easiest, yet it is more necessary than ever, for Hope is the pillar of the world, and the safe haven for the blessed. Allow love to make you strong, allow faith to make you wise, and allow a connection to something grander than your passions, drive your merkaba vehicle to the home we all have the power to access.

△△△

REMAINING SOFT, DESPITE HARDSHIP

"Oftentimes the most difficult roads, lead to the most beautiful destinations"

It is in understanding what we are unable to do, that we recognize the range and mobility in what we CAN. This underlines the necessity for hardship and challenge, for it is in these moments of turmoil we begin to understand our vulnerabilities, as well as our capabilities. It takes a certain type of individual to look at a situation from an objective yet holistic point of view. Keeping in the back of their mind there is a reason for the perceived calamity, as well as the overarching truth that connects the dots.

It takes patience, it takes persistence, it takes a stern understanding of morality, as well as a precision to implement the said value system in a myriad of scenarios. For it is only in perceived opposition that we learn our shortcomings, and find unique methods to redeem them. It is in opposition we learn that it is pointless to meet force with force. We begin to understand that power resides in repose, and in this resting state, it compounds residually.

We begin to unearth the duality within the human experience, and understand the myriad of ways to transcend such. We learn that the heavier aspects of responsibility are ever present, yet how we approach the said burden is emblematic of who we

TRULY are. It is only in opposition that we understand the dynamic impact of our existence, yet also understand that we are not nearly as "invincible" as we would like to believe. It is in opposition that we understand that we not only need others who share our burden, but are completely capable of manifesting the destiny most amicable to our natures. So in closing, hardships are necessary to not only determine who we are, and what we are made of, but to unlock all we can be, and align with the individuals bearing the same burden.

△△△

JESUS WAS FROM SIRIUS AND EINSTEIN WAS FROM ORION (ORION STARSEED TRANSMISSION)

"Imagination is more important than knowledge."- Albert Einstein

There are Lightworkers within every star system. There have always been individuals who served the light amongst a would be impenetrable darkness. The Orion Star System has always been a constellation associated with wisdom. Orion Starseeds have an uncanny ability to transmute the pain every being endures, into timeless esoteric wisdom.

Orion Starseeds aren't granted the luxury of naivete, they understand just how dark things can be, yet KNOW the light is not only a godsend, but a necessity. No matter the star system one's aligned with, The Council of Light is a conglomerate of like minds driven to liberate, and heal the planet. This has been the role of those aligned with this constellation who have served the light, while some of their kin embraced darkness.

I read somewhere a while back that Jesus was from Sirius and Einstein was from Orion. This didn't make sense then, but makes more sense now. Orion Starseeds innately embody The Law of One, and carry a masterful level of objectivity within their energetic being. This full spectrum view of objectivity, has led to Orion Starseeds being seen in a less than positive light. Their deep level of wisdom regarding far reaches of the universe, can lead to a closed off/surgical first impression. Yet, duality is only dangerous to the soul that believes in the illusion of separation.

At its depths, it explains the mechanics of "The Game" many Earth Souls have fallen in love with. At its heights, a mechanism in which we intuit the personality of our higher-selves. By recognizing hate we learn how to move with, and eloquently express, the all encompassing vibration of LOVE. The Heart is everyone's secret channel, and its goal is not to underplay the wonders of the mind. Its goal is to inform all, that feeling doesn't suppress the mind, IT FREES IT!!!

Despite the far reaches of human consciousness, there is a vibration that supersedes all, and that is, real. Real is the essence of authenticity, a person who accepts themselves for all they are, and what they may become. Real is Reality, based in the roots, the simplest microorganism emanates such, yet it is centered in one's relationship with death. How one were to face death with dignity, and embrace the fullness of their life.

Any human being can emanate this quality, it is not necessary they meditate on hours, or read a bunch of spiritual books. It is garnered only on the experience one has accumulated with the life they've been given. If your knowledge were your wealth, then it would be well earned, and the greatest treasures are not of the gold and silver sort. In order to truly grasp the weight of such a concept, requires a certain level of fearlessness, yet even more vital, objectivity. An area well traveled for the Orion Starseed.

The Orion Energy is rooted in the unification of polarities, and it is in doing so, The Orion Lightworker instills harmony effortlessly. Orion Starseeds understand the necessity of going with the flow, and in the same breath, knowing they are the flow. To know when to breeze through, and when to direct their presence. To know when to build a bridge, and when to build a boundary. The difference between a Thermometer and a Thermostat.

Wisdom is seeing the entire puzzle, and making decisions from the said vantage point. It is submitting to the fact that we are the creator of every experience in our lives. We create difficult circumstances to learn, and to move with the wisdom the said experience provided. Real is not a game, and far too many confuse being street smart, with being real. Real has its layers, and we'd be surprised how many things are real. Yet never underestimate on what being real can provide. So Orion Starseeds, Stay You, Stay Blessed, and Stay Real.

FORGOTTEN REALMS OF CONSCIOUSNESS (INTELLIGENT INFINITY TRANSMISSION)

"Now, what really makes a teacher is love for the human child; for it is love that transforms the social duty of the educator into the higher consciousness of a mission"- Maria Montessori

The human mind is nothing short of a miracle. The way it has, and continues, to evolve points towards its essentiality. Yet its wonders, and hidden magick, reside in chambers of the psyche few get the time to explore. Too often the mind is put to tasks where it must "produce" something, yet the mind's magic unlocks when at ease. When we give our mind the permission to unravel, we begin to marvel at, and explore the fluidity of human consciousness as a whole.

It is within the spaces between thoughts, and daily tasks, that the mind unlocks the treasure all have sought. When we allow time for our minds to recharge, we come into contact with a very precious piece of existence. In this subtle, yet vast space, we commune with consciousness in its purest form.

When in nature, this communion is likened to the Fae realms. The divine countenance becomes most apparent in the said space, as we allow ourselves to be free, & wild within our imaginative state, in turn co-creating experiences that affirm the magic within. Yet oftentimes individuals only receive a glimmer of this profound aspect of consciousness. Usually only feeling the connection in certain places, or only feeling connected to source, when in nature.

It is oftentimes the confines of a four corner room are seen as "less divine", or "less free" than say the great outdoors. Yet this feeling must be abated with the essential knowing, freedom is a feeling established from within. With this being the case it is oftentimes that less desirable settings are a prerequisite to explore the true liberation that pure consciousness can provide.

It is within the confines of our rooms, that we unlock the true treasures of our minds. For when we can sit still, become a vibration, and simply allow our conscious minds to unravel into the absolute, we have indeed explored lost lands. This quintessential attribute of all prevailing forms of consciousness is known as, Intelligent Infinity.

Intelligent Infinity is when one has reached the point of communication of ones subconscious to the point in which it is a fluid dialogue, a sort of automatic learning. You will understand the meaning of "downloading information", for it will be a simple byproduct of your subconscious mind. You will absorb lessons from sheer rest, and will emanate all you learn with each human encounter. You will also become a clear channel to connect and communicate with your galactic families, and higher councils of light. Intelligent Infinity is the gateway to deep space, and the network in which all extraterrestrials are able to communicate. This is done via a free transmission of consciousness. allowing YOUR subconscious mind, to naturally unlock, and unravel, as we allow ourselves to be free of thought.

Yet this can only be enjoyed if one places the proper information to learn of. For all learnings are a distortion of pure consciousness at its essence. Yet it is within the proper distortions, such as healing, or teaching, that we garner qualities and roles that are beneficial to the whole of humanity. Yet, this understanding is more than sufficient, for its sheer acknowledgement will direct those destined for such an experience.

So if one wishes to emanate the energies of Atlantis, Lemuria, & Avalon, one only need look deep into the heart of his mind. For the forgotten realms are within human consciousness.

△△△

THE SEER'S SANCTUARY

"It is always with excitement I wake up in the morning wondering what my intuition will toss up to me, like gifts from the sea. I work with it and rely on it. It's my partner"- Jonas Salk

Throughout history there have always been those with a knack to intuit the unseen. In fact, in times of old, these individuals were sought for their innate peculiarities, and were the recommended council for the village and towns leaders and chiefs. In all honesty, in modern times, what society would define as a "peculiarity", were seen as gifts, sacred gifts ushered from the divine, as a means to lead and inform the people closest to these individuals. Though as "time" has progressed, these individuals have been somewhat erased from written history, yet their struggles, triumphs, and overall wisdom, are intricately woven into our collective memory.

I would like to speak on one distinction of clairvoyant ability/role with great depth, this role being that of The Seer. For this is the gift that has been instilled into my energetic signature since the age of 9, and despite its innate level of bounteousness in regards to insight, and clarity, it has been coupled with much confusion, misinterpretation, and overall discomfort within the current state of affairs.

In times past The Seer was a full time job. The community understood the individual's innate level of knowing was to be respected, and most of all honored, seeing the individual as the intermediary between fate and destiny. The Seer's abilities enabled them to decipher the potential paths ahead for all who sought their council, as a means to ease one's journey of self. By pinpointing potential pitfalls, and potential pathways one could encounter in there earthly pursuits, The Seer gave others a clearer vantage point in how to go about their conquests, or even something a simple as finding a potential mate. Where The Shaman excelled in the overall healing, and ritually based practices of appeasing various spirits, The Seer was the pathfinder, and guide one sought to determine on what actions must be taken to fulfill their destiny. In exchange for such assistance Seers were given admirable status within the community, as well as what we would consider monetary compensation. This understood exchange led to an overall balanced community, as well as a more whole soul group as most were working to differentiate between fate and destiny by the help of The Seer. Yet given the current times, this is no longer the understood dynamic, leading many BLESSED with this gift, feeling utterly out of place and consequently, plagued with their god given disposition.

Yet I am here to provide others like myself with a clearer path forward regarding this blessing, yet in the same breath, burden. For even in times of old, The Seer understood this dynamic to be both a blessing, and a burden. Despite having the ability of clear seeing/knowing (Clairvoyance/Claircognizance), this heightened level of psychic sensitivity warranted that these individuals live in a way that limited them from the common social practices of the time. This was more so to protect them from "burning the candle at both ends", as well as to provide a safe space in which they could indulge the fullness of their gifts, and the experience of the divine as a whole. Even as "time" has progressed, these necessities persist.

In modern times the crystal ball has been replaced with a television. Through observing presentations aligned with our innate interests, we are able to intuit our own destinies, as well as become aware of the potential pathways for others. The role of Seer has been replaced with Counselor, for our mysticism not need be acknowledged, more so recognized in the regards to helping others find their way as an innate Pathfinder. We will be surprised at just how many respond positively to our distinct way of being, without us necessarily becoming known as "A Seer". The wise are rare yet common, The Seer has super powers no one necessarily needs to see, yet all deserve to feel and grow from. Though we may not have the status coupled with our acknowledgement, we may find we are given something far greater, and it is up to us, to take the time to discover just how grand that may be. So in turn, to all who know they are a seer, have faith in your abilities, take time to intuit the desires of the heart, and most importantly, have faith and trust in what orchestrated the gifts in the first place. For even in times of confusion and discord, we are being cradled by the divine. When things are at their darkest, The Seer burns Brightest.

△△△

SPIRIT WORLD RESIDENCY (MERGING WITH THE INVISIBLY INFINITE)

"Understand what you are being trained for. Analyze the difficult situation you are in and determine the weakness that makes you negative and off-balance. Ask yourself what prevents you from being positive and working your way out of that situation. That is your weakness, and that is the area in which your spirit needs training. That is the lesson you need to learn. Therefore, that is where you will be tested."- Khorshed Bhavnagari, The Laws of the Spirit World

As all matter within the human experience is birthed via the stars, it is only natural for man to aspire to discover his spirit, and or his invisible nature. For it is in the invisible aspects of man's cognitive and energetic functions, that an individual of esteemed fortitude and astute mental dexterity is born, and allowed entry into the realms of the unseen. It is within these realms that man's moral compass is crafted, and it is within these realms, that man communes with that which birthed the cosmos. Any individual on the "Spiritual Path" is truly working towards this end, and if not working towards, honing their precision in such.

The Spirit World like any has its distinct laws and customs. There are many ways to traverse such a terrain and learn the laws associated with such, yet it is only the few daring and astute travelers that discover the treasures this world presents. For much like the world of man, the world of spirit only awards it's bounty to those who give such serious attention, and tireless commitment to unearthing the pearls within. Those who are of the temperament necessary to honor the said laws are given permanent residency, and become representatives of the invisible. These worldbridgers are what esoterica refer to as The Initiates, and Masters.

These titles are not to be taken lightly despite the ease of access to spiritual doctrine in this era. These individuals have been granted a noble rank of achievement, due to their efforts in maintaining spiritual law, and unravelling the mysteries woven into the tapestry of evolution. These great beings have been tested in ways that cannot go unnoticed, for in the depths of human unconsciousness, they emerged brighter, shining the light of creation for all who seek its warmth. This magnitude of mental involvement, and spiritual exercise exemplifies the miraculous. For these Masters and Initiates were, and are, the pinnacle of spiritual achievement within the human experience.

As the Star Soul consciousness, and 5D Earth realization comes to a head, I feel more individuals need to know what they are working towards. The understanding that cannot go overlooked is that all on the said path are working towards permanent residency. For such to unfold, many will need to abandon the notion of what spirituality "should look like", and understand the world they are seeking to become involved with. Ascension is not about hoping to leave Earth, and visit another planet. Though there may be some truth to extraterrestrial lifeforms, and past life memories of varying forms, the essence of this journey is to unearth the inner workings of the realm of spirit, and understand the nature of a physical life on earth. The goal is not to just raise your vibration, yet to achieve the experience of the boundless, and traverse the realm of the invisible with ease. The goal of being your own Guru is noble, yet to do such, we must tap into what the Guru acknowledges as his/her natural state. It is admirable to ascertain one's self mastery, yet we must understand the laws of the invisible game, to become a Master of the invisible board. This is no small feat, and to do so effectively, requires a complete devotion to discovering the truth of our invisible form.

In truth, this can take many years, lifetimes, even ages, to understand the totality of the higher mysteries and achieve permanent residency. The reason this time in human history is being seen as a pivotal period in spiritual evolution, is due to us being in the finality of the Yugas. In the age of Kali Yuga, many individuals will take up their position within the invisible, after stringent lifetimes in the previous ages upholding the spiritual covenant. In the same breath, many are being introduced to The Spirit World, via the ease of informational access via the internet. For many, these days are the beginning, as the Yugas to follow are truly blissful manifestations, designed to nurture the growth of spirit, and magnify the underlying oneness of all things. There is no rush for permanent residency, for to achieve such in this lifetime requires an arduous commitment to the invisible that honestly, not many are prepared for, nor need for their vessels to be filled with ecstasy and light when life ends. Many will look forward to their upcoming lifetimes, as they will sow the seeds of faith they worked diligently towards in the current. There is no rush, yet if one KNOWS this is their last lifetime, what can be done to secure their place in the Invisibly Infinite?

This question is double edged, for in truth, the answer must express the laws, and demeanor of the spiritually adept. Yet it can be surmised as such, "be wise as serpents yet peaceful as doves". The realization requires a dexterous mental interpretation of the energy the spirit world exhibits. It requires a paradoxical illustration to paint the demeanor required to represent the realm of spirit. Be kind, yet be aware. Be focused, yet be surrendering. Be humble, yet be dignified. Be gracious, yet be frugal.

Understand, the energy of our current reality is a reflection of the realm of spirit. To be bound by the physical is hell, yet to KNOW the spiritual, one must understand the dynamism of such a world has laws to formulate its vastness. And these laws can be understood by understanding the laws currently present in our human experience.

There is so much knowledge to pull from as a source of interpretation given the accessibility of the world wide web. A phone is a literal Supercomputer, yet the masses utilize such a device to swipe left or right, fulfill carnal desires, or patch emotional holes via social media. This is not to demean such behavior, yet to point out the range of use a phone can have, and not limit its function to solely personal, or material uses. Those of permanent residency know that knowledge of spirit is the only knowledge there is. This said understanding sculpts all they are, and all they become. So stay blessed, stay humble, continue to learn, and continue to grow.

△△△

TWIN FLAME ALCHEMY & THE PATH OF DEVOTION

"Only once in your life, I truly believe, you find someone who can completely turn your world around. You tell them things that you've never shared with another soul and they absorb everything you say and actually want to hear more. You share hopes for the future, dreams that will never come true, goals that were never achieved and the many disappointments life has thrown at you. When something wonderful happens, you can't wait to tell them about it, knowing they will share in your excitement. They are not embarrassed to cry with you when you are hurting, or laugh with you when you make a fool of yourself. Never do they hurt your feelings or make you feel like you are not good enough, but rather they build you up and show you the things about yourself that make you special and even beautiful. There is never any pressure, jealousy or competition, but only a quiet calmness when they are around. You can be yourself and not worry about what they will think of you because they love you for who you are. The things that seem insignificant to most people such as a note, song or walk become invaluable treasures kept safe in your heart to cherish forever. Memories of your childhood come back and are so clear and vivid it's like being young again. Colors seem brighter and more brilliant. Laughter seems part of daily life where before it was infrequent or didn't exist at all. A phone call or two during the day helps to get you through a long day's work and always brings a smile to your face. In their presence, there's no need for continuous conversation, but you find you're quite content in just having them nearby. Things that never interested you before become fascinating because you know they are important to this person who is so special to you. You think of this person on every occasion and in everything you do. Simple things bring them to mind like a pale blue sky, gentle wind or even a storm cloud on the horizon. You open your heart knowing that there's a chance it may be broken one day and in opening your heart, you experience a love and joy that you never dreamed possible. You find that being vulnerable is the only way to allow your heart to feel true pleasure that's so real it scares you. You find strength in knowing you have a true friend and possibly a soul mate who will remain loyal to the end. Life seems completely different, exciting and worthwhile. Your only hope and security is in knowing that they are a part of your life." - Bob Marley

I was going to write a very well thought out essay on the mechanics and idiosyncrasies of Twin Flame Alchemy yet this quote by Bob Marley says it all. Even with distance, and lack of physical contact, Twin Flame Alchemy brings these simple pleasures to light. It takes some effort, complete honesty with the self, and complete devotion to the flowering of the heart. Not when it's convenient, but every single day. The same devotion we would give a God or Goddess, can be implemented with our Twin Flame. There will be unnavigable waters, there will be intense moments of longing, there will be moments of complete confusion. Yet the confidence to persist in watering the love that opened your heart in the first place is priceless, and brings incalculable rewards.

In eastern cultures particularly India and South Asia, there have been many individuals who have allowed sheer devotion to another individual transform their lives from the inside out. There are accounts where human beings completely devoted to their practice, even begin to share the physical likeness of that which inspired devotion. Miracles manifest in this realm quite foreign to the mind. It is in the place of incalculable sovereignty, within the heart space, that we unravel the mysteries of being, and discover the secrets of love.

With time we begin to transcend the longing for the person in particular, and recognize our longing as an ache to merge with the Divine. In actuality, they are both true, yet as we transcend we begin to understand why the distance was necessitated, yet understand you will ALWAYS love the person who has shown you things you never thought possible. The hardest part to accept is that they also feel the same, even if they are not in the same space to express their devotion. The love was, and is real for both parties. We shouldn't try and bring them closer with our acts of love, nor should we feel as if we are undeserving of their love, yet we should understand how difficult love can inherently be, and allow the multiverse to carry us along the way to our highest potential.

Divine Unions are about honoring the love that opened your heart in the first place, yet discovering what is best for both in the long run. Understand, your beloved may run because they love you so much... Some loves are terrifying not due to any malice, yet the sheer amount of love they encompass. Not everyone desires the miraculous, and it takes an honest individual to accept such, and still water the love with no hopes of a certain return, but due to the understanding of Love as the universal ingredient in all matters of growth, healing, and prosperity.

△△△

THE BOOK OF JOB & SELF LOVE (ANDROMEDAN STARSEED TRANSMISSION)

"I am brother to Dragons and companion to Owls..." Old Testament, Job 29:30

Was gently guided by my angelic guides to read the Bible for the 1st time in my life. It was the above excerpt that directed me to read The Book of Job in particular. Despite being some of the most fantastic poetry I have ever read, it also highlighted personal struggles since my initial awakening in 2012, as well as what spirit has been preparing on the horizon.

Through a 7 year dark night of the soul much like Job there was a time where I condemned God, The Light, and the naivete of those who believed in such. Only to realize how utterly foolish, and honestly silly such a thing is. Through the said trials I have become privy to certain idiosyncrasies of the shadow that most never will have to endure, yet understand these patterns despite how perverse are ONLY SHADOWS. It is in seeing our shadows we understand the fallacies of misconduct, as well as the true nature of those who wish to conceal what is Sacred.

Just like Job we can become so wrapped up in our personal narrative of suffering and injustice, we fail to see the wider vantage point of our experience and the necessity of such discord. Though I do not feel that God is a being casting lots with the adversary to test his loyal supplicants, I do understand that our initial confusions on God do create a greater depth and reservoir for our eventual cosmic unfolding. The perspective of Job in the story is beyond understandable, as well as human, yet what the story failed to illustrate despite breathtaking imagery is simply, Self Love.

The concept of Self Love has seemed to elude some of the most profound prophetic, and poetic works. For God & Love appear as entities beyond the reach of humanity. Yet Self Love cannot be caught, or put into a bottle. It can only be nurtured and allowed free expression despite external circumstances. If Job would have had a deep love for his circumstances, his words may not have reached such bewitching heights, and if I would have understood the importance of Self Care earlier in my journey, I wouldn't have had such turbulent initiations of Spirit.

I remember reading that one of the main lessons Andromedan Starseeds are here to learn is Self Love, and as I read the words scribed in The Book of Job I understood far too well what was being uttered, as well as how far I have traveled from such initial turmoil. The feeling of being completely cut off from source and society has subsided, yet its flowering will need continual watering on my behalf. In the same token, the aloneness I have found much Solace in is designed to be shared with others, for within this space of softness and sanctity, resides the jewels of comfort Those I care for desire.

It is to my current understanding that Andromedan Starseeds in particular can really learn and grow from The Book of Job. Many of the struggles we face in regards to isolation, and feeling so far from home (2.56 million light years) is mirrored in this one tale. There aren't many Starseed collective readings for us, our guides are very silent yet ever present, and even within the Starseed communities we feel a tad distant from all the "action". It wasn't until recently that I realized that we are honestly BECOMING our guides. The ways we interact with the collective, and those we meet is emblematic of the wisdom we carry from the galaxy we call home.

So in conclusion, so much of the Starseed journey is mirrored in the stories of old. Yet what the stories seem to miss is the inherent closeness of that which they seek in the heavens. God is not above us, yet at our core, at the very heart of our being. Therefore, Love intensely, and shower such love with immeasurable support and affection. And even when God is at the heart of your being, still look up at the stars.

△△△

THE NIGHT LIGHT-WORKER

"It has been said that there are 3 categories of people who are active in the night. The mentally afflicted, the pleasure seekers, and the enlightened"

The following quote is a contemporary translation of a timeless understanding popularized in eastern yogic traditions. This activity includes yet is not limited to the dream time. As a Night Light-Worker ones downloads, light codes, and service will be heightened when the sun has set. This does not necessarily limit their activity when the sun is up, yet does highlight the reality that their most profound insights, and overall productivity will be conducive at night.

At a glance the above interpretation can seem perplexing. How can one be asleep, yet performing light work? How can the time when most are asleep be my designated time of Earth Service? In truth, there are many mysteries that cannot be understood through the logical mind, yet I will attempt to add light to a theme that has proven true for me, and many others.

The first question can be answered very simply, when you Awaken you are never really asleep, only at rest. In this state we are granted the ability to transcend the limitations of the body, and psyche allowing The Night Light-Worker to perform silent miracles for those they contact in the dream state. Yet as was stated earlier this activity is not limited to the dream time, a Night Light-Worker can also be consciously active at night.

Whether this be due to the nature of their work, or simply a time they are most alert and attentive to the currents of Spirit. There was around a 3 year period where I preferred to work the 10PM-6AM shift at local gas stations. This time was often avoided by many gas station clerks for obvious reasons, yet I felt quite at ease in such a space. It was quiet most of the time, I always encountered interesting characters, and it allowed me the solitude necessary to be creatively myself, and eventually led to the first chapter of my book "Tears of The Dragon". Over time I began to view any gas station where I was working, as a lighthouse for the weary and lost traveler. This intention alone carried an immeasurable value, and though I no longer work the night shift, I still carry a very alert state of being when the sun has set. There are still nights of deep dreamless sleep, and even nights where the dreams are mere splashes on a hazy backdrop, yet my presence is most acute in the nighttime. I generally wake up after midnight in 2 hour intervals, and this is not due to being restless, yet a heightened state of awareness. There are even times where I feel I need to recharge in between sleeping to refuel for a more in-depth journey in the dream space. Quite perplexing to say the least, yet quite liberating in terms of perspective.

The second question can be answered with the following in mind, when the outer world is at rest it is most likened to the timeless dimension. When the world around you enters the sleep state they have a greater access to the world the awakened know as reality. In truth, the sleeping state is more aligned with the formless reality than anything else humanity can currently draw from. With this being the case we are given the ability to heal, and share our wisdom with those in need via the dream state. There have been dream journeys where I have taught entire groups of children about the home planet of Lyra since its destruction, as it being the progenitor race of many Andromedan Starseeds. There have been dream journeys where I am guiding an individual I only had brief contact with, on a voyage through their own inner space, unlocking the necessary doors having traversed the said path already. There are even times those I haven't spoke to in quite some time, contact me as their fully realized self as a means to shed light on the current disconnect. Despite these profound experiences, I do not reach out to the people and inform them of such, for I understand that the dream time has yet to catch up to their current life situation. Yet with retrospective, I am able to see the underlying meaning of such experiences.

Light-work is not designed to be a glamorous exploit, most if not all is done in silence. It is designed to unlock doors for others as a means to ease the process of their self realization, and more times than not it can be quite thankless. For in truth, it does not necessitate an accolade only an understanding of the divine nature within all of creation. There is an African Proverb that states, "The night brings wisdom". This timeless truth is epitomized by The Night Light-Worker, for we are the wisdom the night brings.

SHHHH, OR SHARE (A STARSEED'S NEED FOR CHANNELING)

"Every thought is a creative energy that moves the universe to action." - Réné Gaudette

As the above quote illustrates, thoughts hold an immense sway on our personal lives as well as the Cosmic Tapestry as a whole. Though it is imperative to have a silent mind as a means to commune with the majesty of the wordless dimension, it is also just as pertinent to channel wisdom from the said realm as a means to connect the dots for ourselves and others. In truth to be able to accomplish such is a timelessly treasured gift that many aspire. And in actuality, all truly do have access to such if they only believed.

The last two statements have been my gripe regarding this gift known as channeling. I ask myself frequently how much of it is actually my mind, or ego wanting to appear knowledgeable to others? How much of such is actually true, or even necessary in regards to enlightenment as a whole? I look at the Masters of the past and present, and wonder how much more could even be shared regarding an age old truth. Aren't words merely signposts for the wordless experience of divinity? Isn't silence the closest thing to God, and aren't all words mere poor translation?

All of these questions are indeed healthy, and utterly necessary in order to channel clearly. Yet these questions and their answers are not a deterrent of the channeling experience, they only paint the experience of enlightened masters, not all that have ever walked the planet. Every master whether noted in history, or etched in the landscape, had a teaching, and the masters linked to channeling were able to connect others to their divinity through the assistance of a guide, and or star collective.

Though there has always been a need for spiritual teachings to highlight the necessity of silence and quietude, this truth has more to do with a silent mind, not a stoically mute figure of passionless expression. Teachings of the east highlight an individual who is dispassionate regarding their life situation, not the immensity of life and God as a whole. With this being said, the still pool of awareness is where the channeler draws their insights, and in doing so, is able to provide wisdom for themselves and others. The wisdom does not come from them, nor the mind, rather it is expressed through them via the totality, and carries a distinct energetic signature given the beings assisting in their evolution, and the transmission being emitted.

Given the current state of affairs regarding the globally recognized ascension process, and the evolution of the planet we know as Gaia, the need for Starseeds to share what Spirit brings them as a means to grow and assist others in their growth is essential. This is for countless reasons, yet is specifically so Starseeds can provide context to a currently uncharted and yet to be widely recognized phenomenon. The spiritual modalities of earth's current spiritual systems are to be learned from, yet what Starseeds have the ability to tap into are modalities thousands of years ahead of such. It is encouraged that we lean on the insights of the past as a means to ground a Supramental experience, yet not depend solely on one teaching in particular. The teachings of the past are to ground us, yet we all must know we are accomplishing something most masters could only write off as wonder given the times they were born. Their teachings highlight the human condition as a whole, yet the Starseed experience is rooted in a Supermind, and a DNA structure that supersedes current spiritual logic despite its best efforts. This is not to write off what has been accomplished, I strongly encourage all to take the time to digest the material of the teachings of those prior. Yet understand, we are not limited by any teaching nor superior. All spiritual experiences are cosmic in nature, yet the Starseed is gifted with the ability to receive particulars, to questions once thought impossible to answer.

So in conclusion, I encourage all of us to learn from our Star Families, have faith in what can be accomplished, believe that we are capable of helping ourselves and others in ways that exceed our current imaginations, and allow the Masters of past and present to ground an experience that surpasses even their understandings. I had a dream last night and as I was talking to a friend I said with a smile "The Andromedan's won't leave me alone". Now tell me if that doesn't sound like love, or like family.

△△△

THE PATH OF SOLACE, & THE DARK ARTS PRACTITIONER (STARSEED MISSION TRANSMISSION)

"What is a good man, but a bad man's teacher. What is a bad man, but a good man's job"- Lao Tzu (Tao Te Ching)

The above quote has been a staple in my cosmic unfolding, as well as a mental illustration that paints the energy of those who walk the path detailed in the title. It wasn't until recently that I was able to gain a much needed context on my Soul Mission, as I read Steve Ahnael Nobel's free e-book "Starseed: Wake Up and Get On Track". In this book it details 6 categories of Soul Missions Starseeds tend to implement. These categories being, Lightworkers & Healers, Earthworkers & Bodyworkers, System Busters, Technical Innovators, Dark Arts Practitioners, & Soul Awakeners. It is also detailed that we are naturally drawn to more than one path, yet due to our life experiences and dispositions, one path will call to our soul in a way that feels necessary. This channeling is to detail the idiosyncrasies and indicators of a path I have been walking my entire life, yet did not have the context to express such until reading Steve's book. Such a revelation points to the need to lean on the insights of those within the

Starseed Community, no matter how displaced one may feel, and displacement is a common feeling for The Dark Arts Practitioner.

At first glance the words Dark Arts Practitioner feel off-putting, and counterintuitive of the ascension journey. In a spiritual process defined by light and love, the term itself feels shady, and or dubious. Yet what many including myself fail to understand, is that the love shines brightest in the dark, and despite misperceptions, a Dark Arts Practitioner's Soul Mission is to highlight the necessity for Light and Love in all aspects of the human experience, especially the aspects many would write off as beneath them in the Ascension Process. True grace embraces the unlovely and unlovable, and one with this soul mission distinction is urged to take a path very few travel as a means to pacify the pain of those unaware of their inborn sanctity, and neutralize the forces that dwell in the dark.

The mission itself is to meet unappealing energies at eye level as a means to understand their unconsciousness, and find unique ways to heal ourselves and others from the traps set by those wishing to inhibit the ascension process. This is done by a profound sense of empathy, understanding that no individual is their unconscious pattern, rather a by-product of not understanding the soul's majesty. This is not to say that we are to submit to their distasteful ways of perceiving creation. Psychic Self-Defense is a natural ability honed by the Dark Arts Practitioner, and life experiences point to the necessity to protect one's psychic space. Yet how such is implemented is done via a soft touch, rather than a guarded and aggressive demeanor. I have been placed in many life or death psychic scenarios, and urge extreme caution when walking the said path. Yet what has been learned is that there are far more efficient and supporting ways to protect one's psyche, and uplift creation as a whole.

These ways are numerous, yet I would like to point to methods that have been essential in my personal journey in hopes my experience can assist others in their cosmic unfolding. The title illustrates the path in its entirety, for solace should be anyone's aim if they have encountered the darkness in its totality. The definition of Solace is comfort or consolation in a time of distress or sadness. Behind the mask of all egoic dysfunction, no matter how grotesque, is a scared and wounded child. With this timeless truth, egoic dysfunction should be met with gentleness and understanding. We must desire peace more than any would-be aggressor desires conflict, and rest in the knowledge that if defense is necessitated, it will occur naturally without us necessarily having to prepare for such. In truth, we cripple our capability for compassion by treating others as an enemy to be overtaken. War as an energy isn't beneficial, yet a Dark Arts Practitioner learns the profound essence of peace by understanding the energy coined as war. The mind is only weaponized to learn that it serves a far greater function. For a still and clear mind can ultimately serve as a sanctuary for all it encounters.

This is upheld by developing a strong filter for the information & energy we invite into our inner sanctums. This seemingly simple task is only mastered by previous lapses in judgement, and or perceived ability. Though the Dark Arts Practitioner has an uncanny ability to alchemize darkness, this gift should not be implemented on a whim, only out of necessity. In truth, 5D earth necessitates we make the conscious decision between Love & Fear. Despite our abilities this has to be learned via trial and error. The discernment between what activities must be abolished, and what activities have the potential to be transmuted into love can be tedious, and at times feel very self defeating process, yet is necessary, and gets easier with the conscious communion with our spirit teams.

So in conclusion, The Dark Arts Practitioner is not a devious wizard bewitching those who prove troublesome, it is actually quite the opposite. If one is called to this path, really take the time to lean on the Starseed Community as a means to unlock the sanctity such a mission presents. My advice to myself and others would be to integrate the shadow, yet focus on the inner child, focus on the light body. Do not feel that you are cut off from those who have not seen the darkness in its entirety, nor feel ashamed for being a little edgy in regards to your understanding of the Ascension Process. Take your time, and with time and conscious remembrance, we all make it to the other side. Think of the character Professor Snape in the popular book and film Harry Potter. He was a Defense Against The Dark Arts Teacher, he was perceived by students and audience as dubious, yet in the end it was revealed he was protecting the main character, as well as doing it all for Love. Our journeys have no need to be so extreme, yet there is always some wisdom gained by loving the light, by knowing the dark.

ENLIGHTENMENT & THE JOURNEY HOME

"Enlightenment must come little by little - otherwise it would overwhelm."- Idries Shah

The above quote illustrates the magnitude of presence responsible for all we encounter on the earthly plane, as well as Spirit's way of revealing itself to the ardent seeker of a boundless existence. For the magnitude of that which we coin as God is so vast, that even a glimpse of such can overtake the most grounded of spiritual seekers. The following document will be an attempt to express an experience that has shaped every aspect of my being, in a hope to share my experience, as well as provide much needed context for myself and others. It is my humblest intention to make this essay my last, for as I continue to humble myself to the magnitude of existence, I wish to speak less on such, for only the wordless capitulates what all of creation aspires, Union with The Divine.

It all started on a day not much different than any other. At the time I was pursuing a career in music. I was 19 years of age, and was just beginning to unearth the modalities of spiritual insight. I didn't have much guidance aside from my own, and I had an in-depth understanding of the power of imagination. At the time I had an "idea" that each song on my demo tape would express a particular ecstatic state. Little did I know of the countless unnamed yogic masters before me who understood the said experience, yet as many would say "There's no fool like a young fool".

On this day in particular we had finished the project, and as a means to celebrate decided to just "zone out" and listen to the music front to back. The lights were turned down, the music was played loud, and I lay on my back, eyes closed, taking in every vibration the music emitted. It was around the 5th or 6th song that something began to happen, I felt my body expanding. First this happened slowly and then it began to happen at a rate I could not even begin to explain. It was as if my entire being was being enveloped by something so incredibly vast that time, thought, and meaning were completely lost. The presence began to expand until it reached a zenith, a climactic explosion of unwavering bliss. This experience happened within the company of others, yet I knew I was completely alone in such a realization.

Yet as the above quote surmises this experience should happen little by little or else it will overwhelm. Before this realization I had experienced private spiritual experiences, yet with very little context I wrote them off as "good trips". Yet the following experience stood alone for I wasn't under the influence of anything aside from the vibrations of the music. This experience also led to a misinterpretation of the source, for I felt it was music that brought the said realization, when in actuality it was merely the medium source utilized to show me the sheer ecstasy of living.

After such a climactic rise came an ego shattering, and quite terrifying fall. To reach the heights of god realization comes with a humbling realization of our current life situation, as we begin to understand our aloneness in recognition of such an experience. I detail the said experience in the first chapter of my book "Tears of The Dragon". Yet I want to truly highlight that this experience went through a gradual deepening over the years, as more opportunities to integrate became apparent as I was coaxed to release the behaviors and situations that were comfortable, yet ultimately detrimental to my cosmic unfolding.

After the initial experience I spent 6 years looking towards a future in music as a means to "cement my experience in the minds of others". Only to fall even deeper into the arms of the divine in 2018, where a sacred honor was accepted, and a realization of just how little is to be known. I have attempted to externalize my experience via books, music, career choices etc, only to recognize that the only aspect of the ascension journey is to anchor the macrocosmic existence in the everyday, in the eternal now. The experience in itself is what is Sacred, and this can only be appreciated in a total acceptance of the present moment. I personally feel there is truth to extraterrestrial life, as well as the magic of various realms, yet understand that the only thing we truly aspire is union with the divine. The experience is available to everyone who walks the planet, and carries unique expressions for each individual, yet it is ultimately the same experience, individualized to our unique vantage points.

The context we find in our experience is integral to how we show up to those unaware of their inborn sanctity, yet it can only be appreciated by complete acceptance of the present moment. If we "arrive" at enlightenment, we are only aware of our union, there is no end goal, nor is there a "better future". Only a profound acceptance of the now moment, and a distinct need to assist others in understanding their profound impact on all of life. An enlightened individual is just like everyone else, walking, talking, breathing. Yet what is understood is that they are an integral part of the divine tapestry. This integral part doesn't mean larger, rather the profound subtlety of the grain of sand, amidst an unfathomable endless ocean of ecstatic delight. It is encouraged that each of us lean on the insights of the masters of the past, and understand that these beings who understood The Divine as the only aspect of the human experience are the ancestors we seek to contact. There are countless unnamed masters, and the ones named are only so because spirit desired such. Do not feel enlightenment will bring wealth or status, it will only direct you to where you are most needed.

So in conclusion, I just wanted to share an experience, and realization that is designed to help myself and others find peace in the present moment. I intend for this to be my last essay, for I have spent many years attempting to shed light on an aspect of experience that can only be appreciated via the wordless. It is said that Enlightened beings can accomplish many supernatural feats, and though I have discovered such to be true, to control one's mind is far more beneficial, and far more difficult. Blessings to all who read this post, and may more individuals understand that home is not necessarily a distant destination, but resides in the present, eternal now.

Namaskaram

△△△

ABOUT THE AUTHOR

Jameel Shaheed

Jameel Shaheed, Born May 18, 1993, in Charlotte, NC, yet Matthews, NC has been his home for the majority of his life. A precocious individual, yet a devoted student of the mystical, an avid embracer of nature, and an astute observer of the things most individuals miss. He wrote his first book "Tears of The Dragon" in 2019, which insights led to the journey of his latest works, ""Night Sky Silk", "The Windowpane of Eternity", "Leylah's Library: Channeled Writings of The Andromedan Council". Inspired by the poets of the past, his pen is guided by those who have attempted to explain the unexplainable. If one event were to surmise his devotion to the mystical it would be, his "existential crisis" happened at 9 years of age. An event that generally only arises late in ones life, has shaped his many insights on life, as well as his place in the world as a whole.

BOOKS BY THIS AUTHOR

Tears Of The Dragon

The following is a concise handbook of my experience and spiritual insights. It is designed to be succinct and easily applicable to daily life, opposed to the long-winded spiritual textbooks to date. The material's brevity is so the content can be revisited throughout ones life, and to ultimately serve as a compass as we all journey home.

The Windowpane Of Eternity

A succinct set of poems illustrating the beauty, and struggles of True Love. These poems are merely a snapshot in time of the limitless ecstacy woven within our human experience. It is designed to unlock, and nurture the incalculable sovereignty of the reader. Within are 25 poems attempting to simplify the immeasurable. The fluid and consistent rhyme patterns are designed so that the words are easy to follow, as well as pleasant to the ear. Of the many topics that deserve brevity, Love is of the most deserving. Allow love to paint the tapestry of the heart, and allow the sanctity of such a love further your purpose on this earth.

Night Sky Silk

Pure poetry of the heavens, designed for meditative reading. The following transmission takes rather heavy spiritual perspectives, and compartmentalizes the content in a way that is easily digestible, and applicable to daily living. Flashes of creative expression harmonize with new age concepts, in a fluid representation of divinity. Most of all this text is a DNA activation for all who read its context, restructuring the DNA to our celestial counterparts, Enjoy!

Made in the USA
Coppell, TX
12 May 2021